Strange Science:
PLANET EARTH

▼

Q.L. PEARCE

Illustrated by Bernice Mascher

Reviewed and endorsed by
Lauri Reed, consultant,
Department of Earth and Space Sciences,
University of California, Los Angeles

TOR

A TOM DOHERTY ASSOCIATES BOOK
NEW YORK

For Kerstin
—Q.L.P.

With gratitude for the support of family, friends,
students, and coworkers as they stood on the
sidelines cheering me on.

—B.M.

NOTE: If you purchased this book without a cover you should be aware that this book is stolen property. It was reported as "unsold and destroyed" to the publisher, and neither the author nor the publisher has received any payment for this "stripped book."

STRANGE SCIENCE: PLANET EARTH

Copyright © 1993 by RGA Publishing Group, Inc.

All rights reserved, including the right to reproduce
this book, or portions thereof, in any form.

Cover and interior art by Bernice Mascher
Designed by Heidi Freider and Judy Doud Lewis

A Tor Book
Published by Tom Doherty Associates, Inc.
175 Fifth Avenue
New York, N.Y. 10010

Tor® is a registered trademark of Tom Doherty Associates, Inc.

ISBN: 0-812-52365-2

First edition: March 1993

Printed in the United States of America

0 9 8 7 6 5 4 3 2 1

CONTENTS

IMAGINE A WORLD whose surface is shattered into huge plates of land that collide with each other like bumper cars; a world where mountains spew out melted rock hotter than a blast furnace; a world where a bolt of light from the sky can produce enough heat to bake potatoes in the field where it strikes. Picture a planet with raging storms powerful enough to lift huge objects weighing many tons into the air as if they were paper; with underground caverns so enormous that a 20-story building could fit inside; and with an entire continent that is buried under as much as three miles of ice!

The nine known planets of the solar system hold many marvels, but you won't need a spaceship to see the extraordinary sights mentioned above. They can all be found on our own incredible planet. So turn the page and prepare for a remarkable journey as you explore the marvels of Planet Earth!

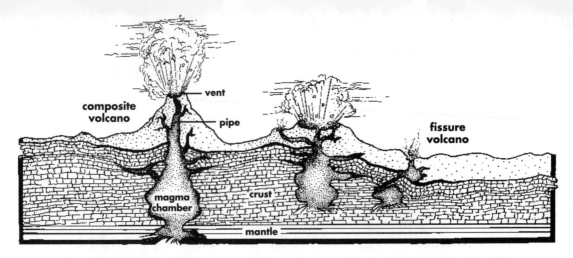

composite
volcano

vent

pipe

fissure
volcano

magma
chamber

crust

mantle

WHAT IS A VOLCANO?

A VOLCANO IS an opening in the Earth's crust through which hot melted rock, called magma, may reach the surface and either blow out as cinder and ash, or gush out as a fiery fluid called lava.

How does the Earth open up to form a volcano? The ground beneath your feet is not as solid as you might think. Earth's crust is divided into at least seven large plates of moving rock. The plates are much like floating rafts. A volcano may form at a boundary where two of the plates meet each other. When a land plate meets an oceanic plate, the edge of the denser oceanic plate is shoved downward. Due to the incredible pressure and soaring temperatures beneath the Earth's crust, the lower plate melts. Some of the scorching rock creeps upward along cracks in the crust and melts a path to about 3 miles below the Earth's surface. There it forms a pool called a magma chamber. This is just the first stage of one of the Earth's most astonishing spectacles—a volcanic eruption. In the chamber, a brew of trapped gases and water vapor released from the magma causes the pressure to build. Eventually, the pressure becomes so great that a crack snakes open to the Earth's surface. The contents of the chamber then race upward and spew into the sky in a

UNEARTHLY WONDERS

VOLCANOES ARE NOT restricted to this planet. Olympus Mons, on Mars, is the largest known volcano in the solar system. It is 15 miles high and 370 miles across at its base. The crater of Olympus Mons is 50 miles in diameter.

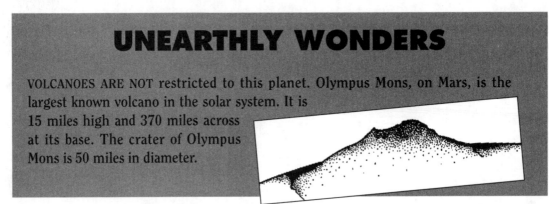

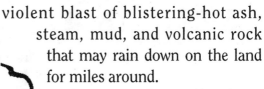

TOUCH!

THE TEMPERATURE OF lava is generally between 1650 and 2200 degrees, or nearly three times hotter than the melting point of lead.

2200°F
1650°F

violent blast of blistering-hot ash, steam, mud, and volcanic rock that may rain down on the land for miles around.

There are basically three different forms of volcanoes. The most well-known form is the composite, or cinder cone, volcano. This type has a single opening, or vent, in the center and is built up of rock, mud, and ash from many eruptions. Fissure volcanoes are cracks in the Earth's surface. Lava may surge out along the entire length of the crack. Shield volcanoes, such as those of the Hawaiian Islands, have more than one vent and are broad and flat. They are formed from thick, fluid lava that erupts fairly continuously over long periods of time.

There are two main types of lava, and they have unusual Hawaiian names. Pahoehoe (PAH-ho-eh-ho-eh) flows quickly. When it becomes solid, it forms ropy sheets. Aa (ah-AH) moves more slowly and has a rough surface when it becomes solid. Both types of lava may flow from the same volcano during an eruption.

pahoehoe   aa

ANOTHER SIDE OF THE DRAGON

VOLCANICALLY FORMED, mineral-rich soils are extremely fertile. In many areas, farmers may grow crops in the shadow of an active volcano.

THERE SHE BLOWS!

THERE ARE NOW about 600 active volcanoes on Earth. These produce a total of at least 20 or 30 eruptions annually. The world's largest active volcano is Kilauea, in Hawaii. (The entire Hawaiian island chain is made of volcanoes, and a new island will soon emerge through volcanic activity.) In the native tongue, *Kilauea* means "much spreading."

Hawaii

Mauna Kea

Mauna Loa

Kilauea

WHAT IS A CAVE?

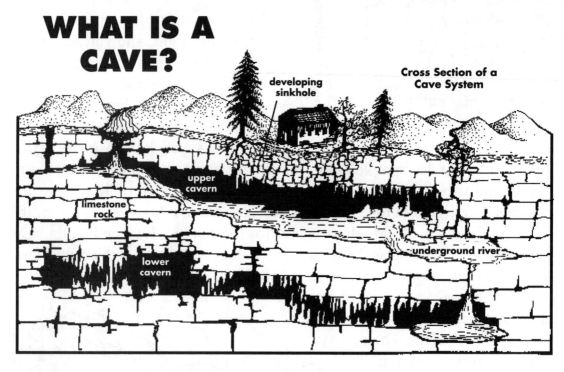

Cross Section of a Cave System

developing sinkhole

upper cavern

limestone rock

lower cavern

underground river

A CAVE IS a natural hollow space in the Earth with an opening to the surface. One centuries-old Nordic tale tells of a strange race of people who lived beneath the Earth and, according to the legend, carved out the planet's caves as entrances to their underground world. The truth is even more amazing. Caves, some of which are hundreds of feet high, are sculpted by the forces of nature, such as wind, ice, and ocean waves. They are formed *inch by inch* over hundreds of thousands—or even millions—of years.

Limestone caves are created by rain. As rainwater falls through the air, it absorbs carbon dioxide and becomes slightly acidic. In areas where the soil and rock are porous, much of this acid-rich water seeps into the ground. Over thousands of years, the acid in the groundwater slowly dissolves the layers of limestone rock, leaving behind openings, or caves.

The same water that carves a cave might also adorn it with fantastic formations. One of

drape stalactite

column

stalactite

stalagmite

cone

stacks

ANIMAL ACTS

IN ASIA, A tiny bird called the edible-nest swiftlet lives in caves near seashores and in rain forests. The bird builds its little cup-shaped nest from layers of its saliva, which hardens into a cradle for its eggs. Once the baby birds have left, people collect these nests to use in a bizarre gourmet treat—bird's nest soup! ➡

edible-nest swiftlet

cup-shaped nest

these is called a stalactite. Once a limestone cave is formed, groundwater continues to seep down through the "ceiling." The water carries dissolved minerals that may drip from the same spot for hundreds of years. As each tiny droplet evaporates, it leaves behind minerals that harden. Drop by drop, stalactites—bizarre "icicles" of rock hanging from the ceiling of a cave—are created. Some drops of water also plummet onto the cave floor, and the minerals left behind build cones, ledges, and stacks, called stalagmites.

A cave may also be filled with water. When the water seeps away, a cave can collapse, creating a "sinkhole" at the surface. The residents of Winterhaven, Florida, learned that the hard way. Winterhaven was built above a large, water-filled cave. As the townspeople drew water from wells to supply their needs, the cave beneath the town was emptied and finally collapsed. One resident watched in shock as a huge tree in her front yard sank into the ground. Now there is a lake in the middle of town that is as wide as eight football fields!

COLOSSAL CAVES

THE WORLD'S LARGEST individual cave is Lobang Nasip Bagus in Malaysia. More than 2000 feet long and 1000 feet wide, this cave could hold seven football fields end to end and is tall enough for a 20-story building to fit inside.

The Mammoth Cave system in Kentucky includes almost 200 miles of passages, on five levels, making it the world's largest cave system. Curious sights await visitors to its corridors. For example, rare creatures such as blindfish and eyeless crayfish live in the darkness of the nearly one-mile-long Echo River.

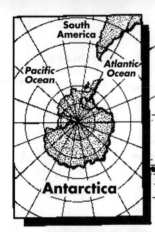

WHAT IS ANTARCTICA?

IT'S A FACT!

IN JULY 1983, the coldest temperature on Earth was recorded at a former Soviet research station in Vostok, Antarctica. It was a very chilly –128.6 degrees.

ANTARCTICA IS THE southernmost continent on Earth. A vast, frozen desert of ice and snow, it is also the coldest place in the world.

When you think of a desert you probably picture a hot, dry land covered with sand and rock. Actually, a desert is any place that receives less than 10 inches of snow, rain, or other moisture per year. Even during the snowiest periods, Antarctica receives an average of less than 4 inches of new snow per year. So, although most of the continent is covered with ice (which, in some places, is almost 3 miles thick), it is still considered a cold desert.

Not all of Antarctica is completely blanketed with ice and snow. There are several valleys of barren rock and sand called dry valleys. Wright Valley is such a place. It is protected from rain, snow, and glaciers by a huge mountain chain, and scientists estimate that rain hasn't fallen there for as long as 2 million years! Yet temperatures in this peculiar valley may still drop to –70 degrees Fahrenheit, and the wind may howl through at up to 120 miles per hour. The sand is actually permafrost—permanently frozen ground. The intense cold and the driving force of the wind have carved

wind-carved rock

Wright Valley

the boulders into bizarre shapes that look like frozen waves on the valley floor. Small streams flowing underneath nearby melting glaciers carry loose sand into the frozen valley, forming miniature sand dunes that ripple across the ground.

There are even a few small lakes in Antarctica's dry valleys. Minerals carried by streams leading to the lakes make the water so salty that, although they may be capped with a thick layer of ice, the lakes do not freeze completely. In fact, the protective ice layer actually helps to keep the salty lake water underneath comparatively warm. The bottom temperature of one—Lake Vanda—has been measured at almost 80 degrees.

You might wonder what sort of animals could survive in such an unusual place as Antarctica. Penguins and seals live along the shorelines of the continent, but they are considered to be mainly creatures of the sea. For a very long time scientists thought there were no animals living on the mainland of Antarctica. However, some insects have been discovered. A wingless fly less than a quarter inch long is the largest known land animal living on the continent!

¼ inch

wingless fly

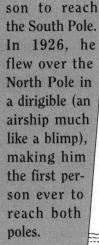

ANIMAL ACTS

MANY UNUSUAL CREATURES live in the icy waters of the Antarctic seas. One very peculiar animal is the giant sea spider. From the tip of one long leg to the tip of the opposite leg, it measures 10 inches across. Its head and body, however, are so small that most of this spider's internal organs are in its *legs!*

BIO BIT
▼

ON DECEMBER 14, 1911, the Norwegian explorer Roald Amundsen was the first person to reach the South Pole. In 1926, he flew over the North Pole in a dirigible (an airship much like a blimp), making him the first person ever to reach both poles.

WHAT IS THE ARCTIC TUNDRA?

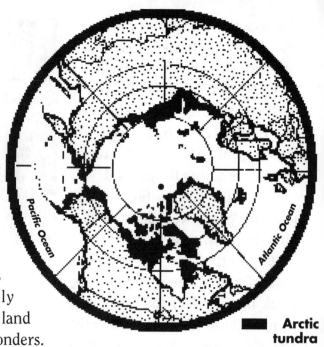

Arctic tundra

THE ARCTIC TUNDRA is a wide band of treeless plains that runs north from the edge of the world's great pine forests (just south of the Arctic Circle) to the shores of the Arctic Ocean. The Tundra is the smallest of Earth's climatic zones—it takes up only about 10 to 20 percent of Earth's land surface. Still, it is a land of many wonders.

During the last ice age, which ended about 10,000 years ago, most of the tundra was covered by huge glaciers. The glaciers are almost gone now, but much of the land they once covered is still permanently frozen! Called

HOW STRANGE!

AS WATER FREEZES, it expands and fills a larger space. As ice thaws, it contracts and fills a smaller space. Tundra soil is constantly expanding and contracting as water in the soil freezes and thaws. This process, called frost heaving, produces some puzzling land formations. In some places, frost heaving forces rocks slowly upward to the surface of the soil. There, the rocks form bizarre, linked circles.

Another odd formation is the pingo. Pingos are earth-covered mounds of ice that may tower 150 feet or more above the surrounding flat plains. They develop when pools of groundwater freeze and the newly formed ice squeezes upward.

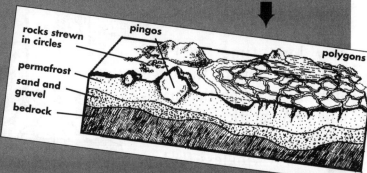

In summer, irregularly shaped patches form when the soil shrinks and cracks. The result are polygons—strange shapes of frozen soil, linked by channels of ice.

permafrost, this frozen soil is, in some places, nearly a mile deep. Even in summer, the air temperature is not much above freezing (32 degrees) so the surface soil rarely thaws more than a few inches down. While this prevents needed moisture in the soil from draining away, it also prevents the growth of plants that need deep root systems, such as tall trees. But some peculiar relatives of willow and birch trees do survive there.

SEE FOR YOURSELF ⬇

TO SEE HOW a pingo forms, fill an empty glass jar with water. Place a layer of aluminum foil on top and press down the edges around the can. Then put the can in the freezer for 24 hours. When you take out the can, you will see that the layer of foil is no longer flat.

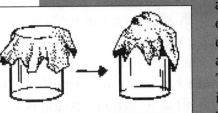

While their branches may spread out over 10 or 15 feet, these dwarf trees rarely grow taller than 5 or 6 inches!

Although much of the tundra appears empty, in spring and summer it is quickly carpeted with fast-growing, ground-hugging plants. Because the growing season is so short, many Arctic plants, such as the purple mountain saxifrage, can sprout, blossom, and produce seeds in less than a month. By comparison, an apple tree, which lives in a more mild climate, does all this over many years!

musk ox

THEY DON'T MIND THE COLD!

THE TUNDRA IS home to such year-round animal residents as the musk ox, Arctic fox, and snowy owl. In spring, other animals arrive, including herds of caribou, as many as 100 different species of birds, and millions of flies, bees, beetles, mosquitoes, and butterflies.

WHAT IS ICELAND?

ICELAND IS AN island country in the North Atlantic Ocean. It is actually a large plateau on top of one of earth's most extraordinary mountain ranges. Called the Mid-Atlantic Ridge, the range is unusual because most of it is at least a mile or two *below* sea level! Along the center of the range is a deep crack in the Earth's crust, where new ocean floor is born. Such a crack is called a rift valley. From deep within the rift, blazing magma wells up. As it comes in contact with seawater, the molten rock sizzles and cools, hardening into tall mountainous ridges on the ocean floor.

About the size of the state of Kentucky, the island nation of Iceland is made up of rock that is more typical of a sea bottom than of a land mass such as a continent. From the rift at its center, Iceland is widening at a rate of about half an inch per year. It is a land of both fire and ice. The "fire" is the hot, molten rock not far beneath Iceland's surface. The island is, in fact, one of Earth's great volcanic regions, with many dozen active volcanoes dotting its surface. The "ice" is in the form of glaciers and snowfields that blanket about 11 percent of the land.

In Iceland's mountainous southeastern corner there lies a huge glacier called Vatnajökull (vat-nuh-YO-kul). Two and a half times the size of the state of Rhode Island, this monstrous glacier has a surface area equal to that of all of Europe's glaciers put together. In the Icelandic

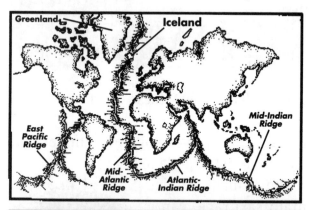

STILL A BABY

ICELAND IS MADE up of some of Earth's youngest rocks. None of them is more than 65 million years old. In contrast, on Greenland, just 185 miles to the west, rocks 3.8 *billion* years old have been found. ➤

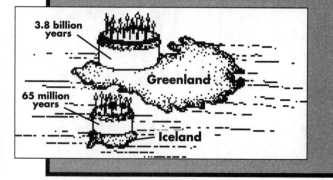

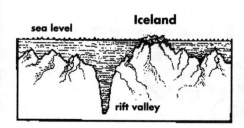

A REMARKABLE BIRTH

ON A BLUSTERY morning in November 1963, a crew member of a fishing vessel reported seeing a burning ship off the southern coast of Iceland. As they neared to assist the ship, the crew found that the source of the fire and smoke was not a vessel, but the volcanic tip of an island in the process of rising from the sea! Within a few weeks, the infant island had risen 567 feet above the water, and it was a little more than a mile long. It was christened Surtsey Island. As its surface cooled, sea mammals crawled out onto its rocks. Birds soon arrived, carrying seeds. By June 1967, Surtsey's first flower—that of a plant known as a white sea rocket— unfurled its petals. ▼

language, *Vatnajökull* actually means "water glacier." The name comes from the rapid melting of the ice that takes place when a volcano hidden under the 3000-foot-thick glacier erupts. The eruption produces floods of warm water that race downhill under the ice and finally burst out onto ice-free plains about 30 miles from the site of the eruption. By the time the water (known as a glacier burst) reaches the plain, it is traveling at about 60 miles per hour and can wash away everything in its path.

WHAT, NO ELEPHANTS?

▼

WHEN ICELAND WAS first settled by Europeans around one thousand years ago, foxes were the largest land mammals on the island.

WHAT IS A GEYSER?

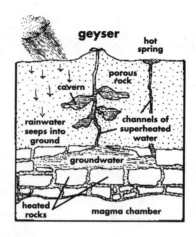

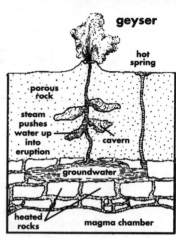

A GEYSER IS a great misty spray, or plume, of steam that erupts from a small opening, or fracture, in the Earth's surface. If you shake up a bottle of warm soda pop, then open it, you'll get a basic idea of how a geyser works. (You'll also make a mess, so this isn't a demonstration that you should perform inside your house!)

A geyser develops in several steps. The first step is when a column of fiery magma inside the Earth rises to within 2 or 3 miles of the Earth's surface and heats the rock layers above. This creates what is known as a hot spot. (In some areas, even the surface soil may feel warm to the touch.)

Step two takes place when groundwater seeps deep into the magma-heated ground. The water may reach temperatures of 500 degrees or more, but because it is under great pressure, it doesn't boil. However, it begins to rise through the rock or through fractures in the rock. Sometimes the water may reach the surface, where it might form a hot spring, a bubbling pool of hot mud, or a jet of steam and other gases that shoots through an opening in a small surface mound known as a fumarole (FEW-muh-rol). Sometimes, however, the superheated water doesn't reach the surface, but enters an underground opening, or cavern, filled with groundwater. The water collects there and eventually boils, producing steam.

Finally, in step three, so much pressure builds up that the steam blasts the water out, and the geyser erupts with a roar

LUNAR EFFECTS

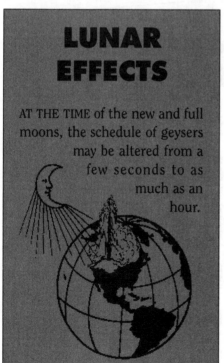

AT THE TIME of the new and full moons, the schedule of geysers may be altered from a few seconds to as much as an hour.

(much like what happens when you remove the cap from a warm bottle of soda pop). Once the outburst is over, the underground cavern fills with water once more and the steam begins to build up again.

The process that leads to a geyser eruption can repeat itself over and over. In fact, though not all geysers spout on a regular schedule, some geysers erupt fairly regularly. Old Faithful, in Yellowstone National Park in Wyoming, is one of the most famous geysers in the world. Located directly over a hot spot, Old Faithful erupts about every 72 minutes. For about 2 to 5 minutes, it spews as much as 12,000 gallons of hot water and steam as high as 184 feet into the air.

Old Faithful

CLEAN ENERGY

THE POWER OF Earth's superheated water can be harnessed to produce clean, geothermal energy (*geo* means "earth" and *thermal* means "heat"). The largest geothermal plant in the world, called The Geysers, is located 90 miles north of San Francisco, California.

ON THE MOVE

FOR REASONS THAT are not clearly understood, as Earth's great crustal plates move over the pockets of magma that produce hot spots, the pockets remain fixed in one place. Because of this, the area of volcanic activity at the surface shifts. The crust of North America is moving westward over the stationary hot spot that presently fuels the geysers of Yellowstone Park. Eventually, over millions of years, the volcanic activity will be centered in Montana rather than Wyoming.

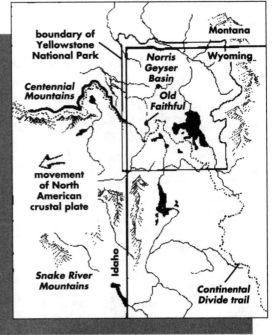

boundary of Yellowstone National Park

Montana

Wyoming

Norris Geyser Basin

Centennial Mountains

Old Faithful

movement of North American crustal plate

Snake River Mountains

Idaho

Continental Divide trail

WHAT ARE THE HIMALAYAS?

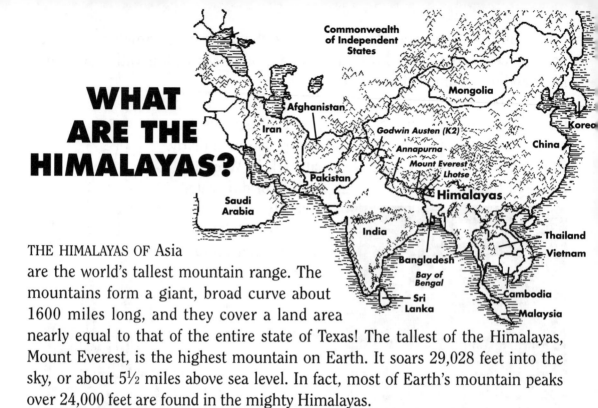

THE HIMALAYAS OF Asia are the world's tallest mountain range. The mountains form a giant, broad curve about 1600 miles long, and they cover a land area nearly equal to that of the entire state of Texas! The tallest of the Himalayas, Mount Everest, is the highest mountain on Earth. It soars 29,028 feet into the sky, or about 5½ miles above sea level. In fact, most of Earth's mountain peaks over 24,000 feet are found in the mighty Himalayas.

Amazingly, this enormous mountain range is the result of a collision! A slow pileup between the subcontinent of India and the continent of Asia took place about 40 million years ago. For 70 million years before that, the land mass that is now India had been drifting northward. Finally, with its way blocked by the Asian continent, India rammed into what is now Tibet. Inch by inch, the northern edge of India crumpled and folded upward into the towering Himalayas. The floor of the shallow sea that had existed between India and Asia was lifted. The collision also pushed up the Tibetan Plateau to nearly 3 miles above sea level. This area had once been an ancient seacoast. Today it is the world's largest, highest plateau (a flat, raised land surface). The average temperature on its dry, windy, treeless plains is not much above freezing (32 degrees).

The climate of the rugged Himalayas is generally severe. The higher one climbs up a mountain, the colder the air becomes. The temperature drops about 3 degrees for every

Collision of Crustal Plates

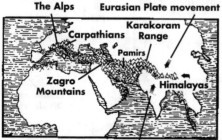

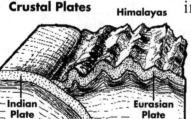

1000 feet above sea level. During the coldest season, the temperature at the top of the Himalayas may drop to minus 21 degrees, and the wind may reach speeds of more than 100 miles per hour. The highest peaks are always covered with snow, and many glaciers lie in the deep canyons and mountain gorges. The largest of these glaciers, Gangotri, is 20 miles long.

ANIMAL ACTS

ONE-THIRD OF Earth's animals that live in the mountains are found in the Himalayas. These animals include three types of mountain goat: the ibex, the markhor, and the wild goat. Another resident is the rare and beautiful snow leopard. This animal can live as high up as 19,000 feet above sea level. It is protected from the cold temperatures by a thick, black-spotted coat of soft, whitish fur. The hair between the leopard's footpads is very long, so even the bottoms of its feet are padded by warm, soft fur.

snow leopard

BIO BIT

route of successful ascent of Mount Everest

reaching the summit

AFTER MANY attempts, the mighty Mount Everest was finally climbed on May 29, 1953, when two members of a British expedition—Sir Edmund Hillary of New Zealand and a Nepalese mountaineer named Tenzing Norgay—reached the summit. Hillary was knighted for his effort that very same year. Between 1955 and 1958, he led the New Zealander team that was part of a trans-Antarctic expedition. He reached the South Pole on January 4, 1958.

HOW STRANGE! ➡

SCIENTISTS KNOW THAT a shallow sea once existed between Asia and India millions of years ago because of what the sea left behind—fossils! Tiny fossil creatures from this ancient sea can be found not at sea level, though, but in rocks high in the mountains!

fossil sea creatures

WHAT IS THE GRAND CANYON?

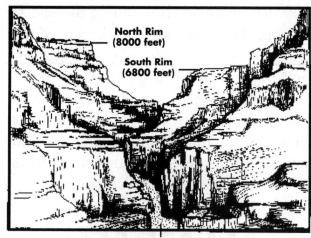

North Rim
(8000 feet)

South Rim
(6800 feet)

Colorado River

THE GRAND CANYON of Arizona is a long, deep canyon or opening in the Earth's crust that was cut mainly by the fast-flowing waters of the Colorado River. The Grand Canyon covers 2000 square miles and stretches along 277 miles of the Colorado River. It is as much as a mile deep and between 4 and 18 miles wide.

The history of the formation of the Grand Canyon begins about 30 million to 40 million years ago. At that time, the movements of the Earth's great crustal plates squeezed the land in that area upward into a huge, slightly dome-shaped plateau. At first, the ancestor of the river that was to become the Colorado flowed along the eastern side of the plateau. Meanwhile, on the western side, great streams of runoff rainwater were wearing deep channels across the plateau toward the east. Between 2 million and 10 million years ago, the channels broke through to the river on the eastern side. That river then changed course to follow a new westward path, and the present Colorado River was born.

Since that time, the river has continued to cut into the still-rising land. As it does so, the river exposes ancient layers of rock, such as shale, limestone, sandstone, and granite. The deeper the river cuts, the older the layers of rock that are exposed. At a place called Granite Gorge, the deepest point of the canyon, the rock that borders the riverbed is as much as 2 *billion* years old!

Washington

Oregon

Nevada

California

Utah

Arizona   Kaibab National Forest

Nevada

Grand Canyon National Park

Lake Mead

Colorado River

Lake Powell
Colorado River

Little Colorado River

Wyoming

Nevada

Utah
Lake Powell

Colorado River

Colorado

San Juan River

Grand Canyon

Colorado River

Little Colorado River

Arizona

New Mexico

Because of the Grand Canyon's great depth, weather conditions from the bottom to the top of the canyon vary widely. At the bottom, the canyon is warm and desertlike. In fact, in summer the temperature can reach up to 120 degrees in the shade. On the same day, the temperature may be as much as 35 degrees cooler in the forests of Ponderosa pine on the top rims of the canyon. Towering high above the Colorado River, the North Rim of the Grand Canyon is cooler and on average about 1200 feet higher than the South Rim.

A COLOR!

ONE ANIMAL THAT lives only in the Grand Canyon is the pink rattlesnake. It is rarely seen, probably because its dark, pinkish-red skin helps it to blend in with the reddish desert rocks among ➤ which it lives.

HOME SWEET HOME

BECAUSE OF THE Grand Canyon's wide range of climate and environment, there is also a wide range of animal life. It is home to deer, cougar, bobcats, ring-tailed cats (which are closely related to raccoons), coyotes, porcupines, lizards, bats, and scorpions. Some of the animals, such as the beautiful black-and-white Kaibab squirrel, are found nowhere else in the world.

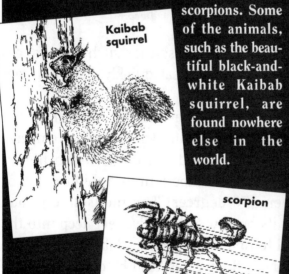

Kaibab squirrel

scorpion

LATE BLOOMER

ONE AMAZING PLANT that grows in the Grand Canyon is the century plant. During its 10- to 30-year life span, it blooms only once—at the end of its life. The plant sprouts a central stalk that may grow as much as 10 inches in a day, reaching a height of between 10 and 40 feet. Finally, clusters of waxy, cream-colored flowers blossom at the top of the stalk and produce seeds from which new plants will grow. Once this job is done, the century plant dies.

WHAT IS THE SAHARA?

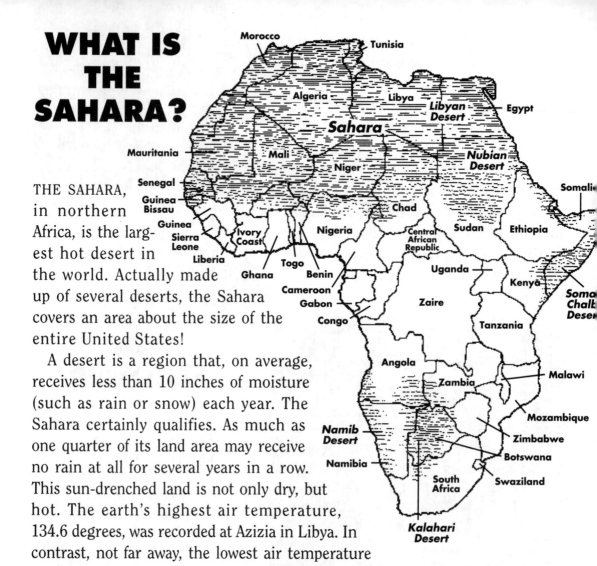

THE SAHARA, in northern Africa, is the largest hot desert in the world. Actually made up of several deserts, the Sahara covers an area about the size of the entire United States!

A desert is a region that, on average, receives less than 10 inches of moisture (such as rain or snow) each year. The Sahara certainly qualifies. As much as one quarter of its land area may receive no rain at all for several years in a row. This sun-drenched land is not only dry, but hot. The earth's highest air temperature, 134.6 degrees, was recorded at Azizia in Libya. In contrast, not far away, the lowest air temperature ever recorded in the Sahara was 20 degrees. The reason for such wide ranges of temperature is that the sand absorbs and loses heat quickly. Very hot days are often followed by very cold nights.

Desert animals have found ways to get relief from the scorching sand during the day. The temperature of the ground can climb much higher than the air temperature—as high as 150 or even 170 degrees! The mouselike jerboa digs its burrow at least five feet deep into the sand to find a more comfortable temperature of about 86 degrees. And by climbing into a small bush, the monitor lizard "cools down"

150° to 170°F

86°F

jerboa

in air temperature close to 120 degrees.

Only about 20 percent of the Sahara is actually covered with sand. Most of it is paved with rock. In some places, rocky outcrops have been carved by windblown sand into odd shapes called yardangs. One of the most incredible rock formations, however, is called desert pavement. It is a layer of flat, pebble-sized pieces of rock that may stretch for thousands of miles across the desert floor. Over the centuries, these pebbles have settled and wedged tightly together to form the desert pavement.

fault

oasis

aquifer

nonporous rock

IT'S A FACT!

REDDISH DUST FROM the Sahara is sometimes carried by the wind high into the atmosphere, where it may drift as far as 2000 miles away. In fact, the red dust has been found on rooftops in Paris, in the snow on the Swiss Alps, and even as far north as Sweden!

The Alps

Europe

PARIS

Africa

Sahara

WHERE ⬆ DOES *THAT* COME FROM?

YOU WOULDN'T THINK there is water in such a desolate desert as the Sahara, but there is. Where does it come from? Rainwater from mountains very far away seeps into the ground until it is trapped in a layer of porous rock called an aquifer (from *aqua,* meaning "water"). The water may travel underground through the aquifer until it reaches a barrier of rock that is not porous. Here the water often bubbles along a fault toward the surface, to become one of the desert's most pleasant areas—an oasis.

WHAT IS DEATH VALLEY?

DEATH VALLEY IS a desert region in California that is 140 miles long and 4 to 16 miles wide. It is a land of extremes and surprises. The average summer temperature in Death Valley is about 125 degrees. A record high air temperature of 134 degrees in the shade was recorded there in 1913, making Death Valley the hottest place in North America.

Death Valley is also the driest place in North America. There is rarely more than 1½ to 2 inches of rainfall each year. Most of the water in the valley is in salt ponds, marshes, and a few scattered freshwater springs. The main sources of water—the Amargosa River, Salt Creek, and Furnace Creek—are often dry!

Besides being the hottest and driest place in North America, Death Valley is also the lowest point in the Western Hemisphere. About 5 miles west of Badwater, California, the land dips to 282 feet below sea level. Amazingly, Mount Whitney, the highest point in the continental United States (that is, not including Alaska or Hawaii), towers just 100 miles to the west. At 14,494 feet above sea level, it is clearly visible from Death Valley.

In spite of the hardships its harsh environment presents, Death Valley is home to a wide range of animals. These include birds, lizards, jackrabbits,

Nevada

SAN FRANCISCO

California

Death Valley

LOS ANGELES

SAN DIEGO

hawk

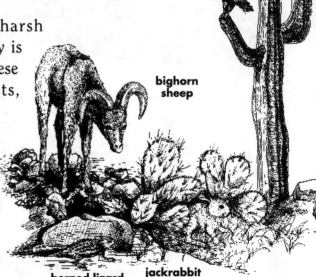
bighorn sheep

burro

horned lizard   jackrabbit

WHAT'S IN A NAME?

IN 1849, 30 prospectors attempted to take a shortcut across the unnamed valley that led to the goldfields of California. They suffered terribly from heat and thirst, and many died. One of the 18 survivors of that ordeal named the desert Death Valley.

desert rats, coyotes, kit foxes, bobcats, hawks, and bighorn sheep. The valley even has a population of wild burros. The burros' ancestors were brought to the area by miners and prospectors in the 1800s.

Plants, too, dot the landscape. Those that can survive on salty water, such as saltgrass and pickleweed, grow at the edges of the salt marshes. Cactus and mesquite thrive in some areas. But the most common plant is the extraordinary, creosote bush. The creosote, which grows up to 10 feet high, doesn't need to reproduce by spreading seeds. Instead, the crown of the plant splits into several sections that bend toward the soil. Each section sprouts its own roots and branches, but each is identical to, or simply an extension of, the original plant. Because of this, some scientists claim that although an individual bush may live for about 100 years, the age of the plant should be determined by the spreading shoots as well. One such group in the Mojave Desert has been dated at 11,700 years of age!

122°F

Devil's Hole pupfish

ANIMAL ACTS

DEATH VALLEY HAS a most unusual native fish. The tiny Devil's Hole pupfish can thrive in water as hot as 122 degrees! It lives in a pool that is 30 to 40 feet wide at the surface and narrows to 10 feet farther down. Groundwater feeds the pool through a slender channel that may be as much as 300 feet deep. The pupfish feed on algae that grow on a rock ledge just a few feet beneath the surface of the water.

WHAT IS THE GREAT RIFT VALLEY?

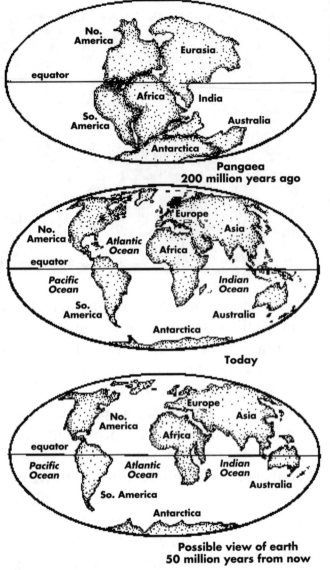

**Pangaea
200 million years ago**

Today

**Possible view of earth
50 million years from now**

THE GREAT RIFT VALLEY of East Africa is an incredible 2500-mile-long valley that runs from the lower end of the Red Sea to Mozambique.

Some 250 million years ago, even before the earliest dinosaurs appeared, the land on Earth's surface was gathered together in one supercontinent called Pangaea (pan-JEE-uh). Over millions of years, this giant continent split into huge sections that slowly drifted apart into the continents we know today. The Great Rift Valley is one of the few places on dry land where people can still witness the same sort of remarkable events in nature that caused Pangaea to split apart.

About 20 million years ago, in an area we now call East Africa, a huge bubble of magma from inside the earth pushed its way up toward the surface. The land above the magma lifted and began to split and crack apart, creating a wide rift that would eventually stretch from what is now Ethiopia to Mozambique. Huge sections of land dropped down, forming spectacular valleys bordered by steep, towering cliffs. In some places, the cliffs rise 2000 feet straight up from the valley floor.

At the northernmost point of the Great Rift Valley is a low-lying region called the Afar Triangle. The bizarre triangle is actually a huge section of seafloor that has been shoved to the surface. Here lies the Danakil Depression, a desert that's 2000 square miles and 400 feet below sea level. This area was once a tiny arm of the Red Sea, but as the land rose, the Danakil Depression was cut off from its source of water. The remaining water soon evaporated, leaving behind a layer of salt. In some places, the salt is 3 miles thick!

Moving south from the Afar Triangle, the rift splits into two arms which join again near the southern end of the valley. Among the many wonders of the Great Rift Valley is Lake Tanganyika, the second deepest lake in the world. It fills a deep, wide opening in the western arm of the rift. Lake Victoria is between the two arms. Mount Kilimanjaro and Mount Kenya, two of the world's largest volcanoes, stand guard over the eastern arm.

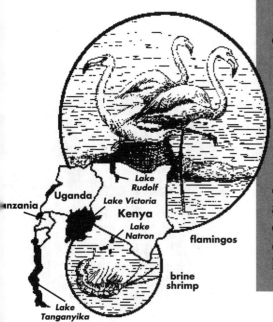

flamingos

brine shrimp

ANIMAL ACTS

ONE OF THE lakes in the Great Rift Valley is 400-square-mile Lake Natron. In some places, this lake is tinted red by bacteria. In other places, algae color the lake deep green or brick red. Lake Natron is fed mainly by hot springs and streams filled with sodium carbonate, a salty substance much like baking soda. The only creatures able to live in this water are certain insects and brine shrimp. These animals form part of the diet of the flamingo, one of the earth's most exotic birds. Where does the flamingo get its bright pink color? From eating the brine shrimp!

WHAT ARE THE GALÁPAGOS ISLANDS?

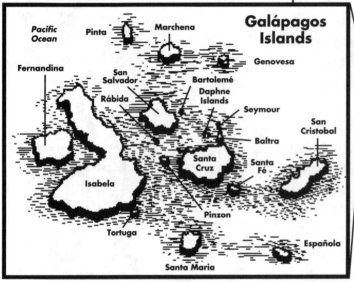

Galápagos Islands

THE GALÁPAGOS ISLANDS are a small group of islands in the Pacific Ocean, about 650 miles from the coast of Ecuador, South America. These islands had a violent beginning. They are the tops of enormous underwater volcanoes that, for at least 5 million years, spouted fiery lava and grew steadily higher and higher until they finally peeked above the surface of the sea. There are 16 main islands as well as many tiny islets. The climate and plant life are different from island to island) and from place to place on the larger islands), with regions ranging from dry lowlands to thick, tropical forest.

The first people to set foot on the Galápagos were most likely Polynesians, though it is not certain when they arrived. The first European discovery of the islands was made by Spanish explorers in 1535. The name *Galápagos* (Spanish for "tortoise") was given in honor of the extraordinary giant land tortoises that still live on several of the major islands.

Since then, the Galápagos Islands have had a very colorful history. During the 17th and 18th centuries, they were known as a gathering place for some of the roughest, fiercest pirates of the Pacific Ocean. In 1835, the famous scientist

HOW RARE!

NEARLY HALF THE vegetation found on the Galápagos Islands is found nowhere else in the world.

Charles Darwin visited the Galápagos. The animals he found there helped to inspire his theory of biological evolution. For example, he studied the beak shapes of finches (now known as Darwin's finches) on the various islands. He noticed that among the 14 different species of this bird that he found, some had strong seed-crunching beaks while others had slender, insect-gripping beaks. Two other varieties even used twigs or cactus spines to dig insects or wormlike grubs out of holes or cracks. Darwin's theory was that all these birds had adapted, or changed, to take advantage of the different food sources on the island where they lived.

Darwin's finches and their varying beak shapes

The Galápagos Islands are famous for their unique wildlife. There are about 80 different species of birds, including flightless cormorants, as well as the world's only sea-going lizard, the marine iguana. The Galápagos Islands are also the only place where fur seals and penguins, commonly found in very cold climates, live at the equator.

marine iguana

ANIMAL ACTS

THE GALÁPAGOS TORTOISE is one of the world's largest living tortoises. Its shell may be more than 4 feet long and the entire creature may weigh up to 600 pounds. There are several varieties of Galápagos tortoises, which differ from island to island and even from one part of an island to another. This remarkable creature is believed to live longer than most other animals on Earth. One individual in particular reportedly lived to be 175 years old!

➡

great land tortoise

600 pounds

WHAT IS A MANGROVE SWAMP?

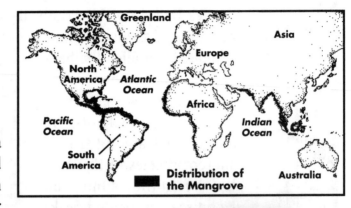

Greenland

Asia

Europe

North America

Atlantic Ocean

Africa

Pacific Ocean

Indian Ocean

South America

Distribution of the Mangrove

Australia

A MANGROVE SWAMP is a forest of special trees called mangroves. They form on shallow mudflats that border calm bays of water, or along the muddy mouths of rivers that drain into warm seas. In such areas, fresh water flowing out from streams and rivers joins and mixes with salt water from the sea. Most trees cannot survive in salty water, but the mangrove tree thrives in it. Extra salt from the water simply collects in the mangrove's long leaves. The salt is then released through tiny openings in the leathery surface of the leaves.

The mangrove's very special roots give this tree a fantastic look. The roots are pyramid-shaped, and they curve downward from the tree's trunk above the surface of the water. Then they enter the water and work their way deep down into the soggy mud to hold the tree securely in place. Long, thin shoots also grow upward from the roots. These shoots make it possible for the mangrove to absorb oxygen from the air.

Mangrove trees usually grow along quiet shores. But when necessary, because of their strong roots, mangroves can easily withstand the force of waves

IT'S A FACT!

MANGROVE TREES MAY grow to be more than 80 feet tall, and a mangrove swamp may stretch as far inland as 60 miles.

new shoot

young mangrove

adult mangrove

and the pull of tides and currents. These trees can even resist very strong hurricanes. That's partly because, over time, sand and mud collect around the tangle of roots. This helps to strengthen the roots' anchoring. It also helps to build up the land along the shoreline. As more trees grow, the land extends farther out into the water. For this reason, mangroves are known as the "mothers of islands."

The seeds of the mangrove tree are also well suited to developing in salt water. These unusual seeds sprout while still on the tree! The seedling is actually a miniature tree. If it falls from the parent tree at low tide, it can sink deep into the mud below and take root. However, if the tide is high and the water beneath the parent tree is too deep, the seedling will float away. That doesn't mean it will die, however. It may travel for hundreds, or even thousands, of miles, protected by its tough, outer covering. When it reaches calm, shallow water, the seedling will take root and begin to grow in just a few days!

STRANGE FRUIT ▼

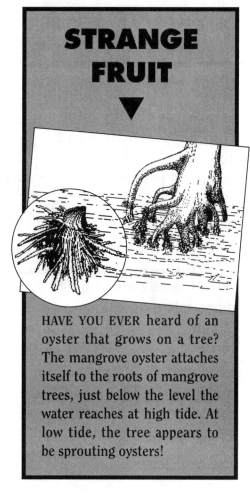

HAVE YOU EVER heard of an oyster that grows on a tree? The mangrove oyster attaches itself to the roots of mangrove trees, just below the level the water reaches at high tide. At low tide, the tree appears to be sprouting oysters!

ANIMAL ACTS

MANGROVE SWAMPS ON the shores of the Pacific and Indian oceans are home to an unusual fish known as the mudskipper. When in danger from other animals in the water, young mudskippers crawl right out of the water and onto mangrove roots for safety! This fish can stay out of water for several hours at a time. That's because it can take in oxygen through its skin! It moves across the muddy shore of the swamp by leaping as far as 2 feet with each leap.

WHAT IS A SALT LAKE?

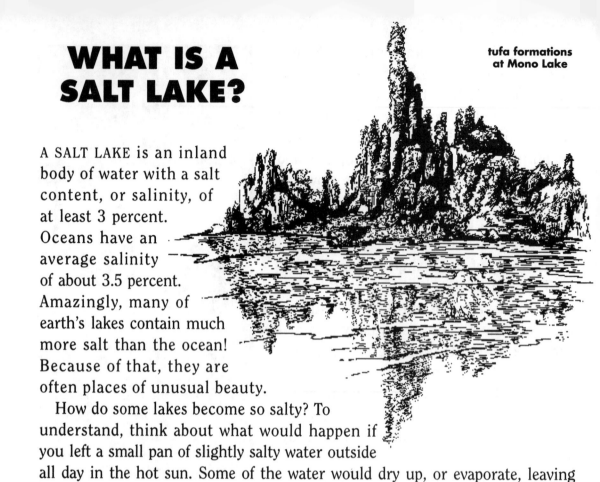

tufa formations at Mono Lake

A SALT LAKE is an inland body of water with a salt content, or salinity, of at least 3 percent. Oceans have an average salinity of about 3.5 percent. Amazingly, many of earth's lakes contain much more salt than the ocean! Because of that, they are often places of unusual beauty.

How do some lakes become so salty? To understand, think about what would happen if you left a small pan of slightly salty water outside all day in the hot sun. Some of the water would dry up, or evaporate, leaving the salt behind. As you added more slightly salty water, it, too, would evaporate, leaving behind even more salt. In this way,

river brings minerals to lake → **river stops flowing and water level drops** → **evaporation increases the concentration of minerals**

the water would become saltier and saltier. Lake water also evaporates, and it also is usually replaced by water flowing in from freshwater streams and rivers. As these rivers and streams rush along, they wear away rocks and minerals in their paths, and, in the form of sand, mud, and dissolved minerals, this often salty material is washed into the lake. In a freshwater lake, much of this material is eventually flushed out through rivers or streams that flow away from the lake. However, when the normal channel of outflow is cut off, the concentration of salts builds up. Over time, water from the lake surface

Great Salt Lake

Lake Bonneville 16,000 years ago

Utah Lake

Green River

Utah

Colorado River

Lake Powell

Sevier Lake

evaporates, leaving the minerals behind. The lake gets saltier and saltier. This is how the largest salt lake in the United States, the Great Salt Lake of Utah, formed. It is all that is left of a huge body of water called Lake Bonneville that, about 13,000 years ago, covered an area twice the size of Vermont! The Great Salt Lake's salinity level is about 22 percent, which is about six times saltier than the ocean!

Freshwater springs beneath the surface of a salt lake, such as Mono Lake in California, may bubble up into it. Dissolved minerals in the spring and lake water then combine to form a hard, crusty material called tufa. The tufa forms into fantastic shapes, and when the water level of the lake drops, these ragged tufa formations are exposed. They look like bizarre castles standing in the salty water.

Mediterranean Sea

Sea of Galilee

Jordan River

Jordan

Israel

Dead Sea

Gaza Strip

SEA OF DOOM
▼

WITH A SALT content of 28 percent, the Dead Sea, between Israel and Jordan in the Middle East, is the world's saltiest lake. The lake is so salty that fish traveling from freshwater rivers into this sea die within moments. This is because the tremendous change in salinity upsets a freshwater fish's internal water balance.

EXTRA!
READ ALL ABOUT IT!

FLOATING IN A lake is an unlikely way to read a newspaper. Still, the waters of the Dead Sea are so dense with salt and minerals that it is nearly impossible to sink in them. A person could relax and read the paper without getting it wet.

WHAT IS LAKE BAIKAL?

LAKE BAIKAL, LOCATED in southern Siberia in Russia, is the world's deepest and oldest lake in continuous existence. The waters of Lake Baikal fill a huge depression caused by a break in the earth's crust. This depression, called a graben, began to fill with water about 25 million years ago. Today the lake is about 395 miles long and between 10 and 50 miles wide. Its surface area is about 12,000 square miles, which is only a little more than one-third the surface area of Lake Superior, the largest of the Great Lakes of North America. But because Lake Baikal is so deep—nearly a mile—it holds as much water as all of the Great Lakes put together. In fact, Lake Baikal holds an amazing 20 percent of all the world's liquid fresh water!

Two underwater mountain ridges cross the width of Lake Baikal. The very tip of one is visible above the surface of the water as the 320-square-mile island of Olkhon. The lake is also the site of an unusual phenomenon that, until recently, had been observed only on the ocean floor. Underwater hot springs called hydrothermal vents occur

Depths of Various Lakes

Lake Baikal · Lake Superior · Lake Michigan · Lake Huron · Lake Erie · Lake Ontario

TAKING ITS TIME

ABOUT 330 RIVERS and streams flow into Lake Baikal. But all this water has only one outlet—the Angara River. If all of the sources of fresh water coming into the lake were cut off, it would take 400 years for this huge body of water to empty.

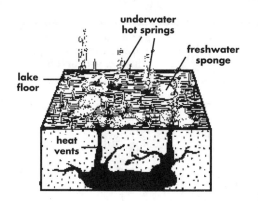

lake
floor

underwater
hot springs

freshwater
sponge

heat
vents

deep in the lake, where magma from inside the earth nears the floor of the lake, warming the rock above. As cold water seeps into cracks in the rock, it becomes superheated. It bubbles back up through the rock at the hydrothermal vents, dissolving minerals from the rock as it goes. This warm, mineral-rich water nourishes many unusual forms of life on the lake floor, including tiny shrimp and colorful sponges that resemble those found in oceans.

ON THE SURFACE

ON STORMY DAYS, waves as high as 15 feet may churn across the surface of Lake Baikal. During winter, an extremely clear, 6-foot-thick layer of ice covers the lake.

ANIMAL ACTS

▼

THERE ARE ABOUT 1,700 kinds of animals and plants in Lake Baikal. More than two-thirds of these are found *only* in this unusual lake and nowhere else, including the following unusual creatures:

• The golomyanka (go-lom-YAN-kuh), an 8-inch-long, deep-water fish, has no scales. About one-third of its body weight is oil. If it is washed ashore, sunlight melts the oil away, leaving only skin and bones behind.

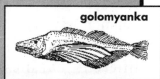

golomyanka

caddis fly

larva protected by pebbles

without pebbles

• The flightless caddis fly, while it is still a larva, has the bizarre habit of covering itself with a case made of mucus and sand pebbles. Before becoming an adult, the insect uses its powerful mouthparts to cut away the case. This fly is "flightless" because, over time, its wings have gradually evolved into tiny "oars." It can't fly, but it sure can swim in Lake Baikal!

• The nerpa, another resident of the lake, one of the world's two types of freshwater seals, is the only seal to live so far inland.

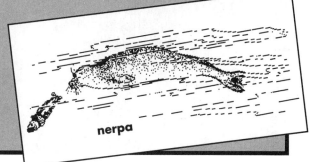

nerpa

WHAT IS A WATERFALL?

series of steps and rapids developing into a waterfall

A WATERFALL IS the sudden drop of water in a river or stream over a ledge or cliff. Waterfalls develop in a variety of ways. One of the most common ways begins when a river flows over rock layers of different hardness. Some layers of rock across the riverbed may not wear away as quickly as others. While rushing water can flow over layers of hard rock with little effect, its force quickly cuts through softer rock, deepening the riverbed. In some places, such as at Niagara Falls, there may be a single level of hard rock remaining. As the water sweeps away softer rock, a single fall develops. In other areas, there may be several rocky layers remaining, forming a series of falls.

Some waterfalls are gentle flows tumbling over small drops. Others are incredibly grand and powerful. The roar of 400-foot-high Victoria Falls of the Zambezi River in Africa can be heard more than 20 miles away, and a curtain of mist rising from these magnificent falls can be seen 25 miles away! Every minute of every day, about 62 million gallons

Victoria Falls (aerial view)

FAMOUS FALLS

EACH YEAR, MILLIONS of tourists travel to view Niagara Falls, making it the world's most visited waterfall. This waterfall is on the Niagara River, which connects Lake Erie and Lake Ontario, two of the Great Lakes. Goat Island divides the waterfall into two sections, or cataracts. Because the Falls are on the border between Canada and the United States, each cataract is in a different country!

Goat Island

Horseshoe Falls

United States

Canada

American Falls

CARE FOR A STROLL?

SOMETIMES IT'S possible to actually walk *behind* a cascading waterfall. Once a waterfall develops, it continues to change. The force of the water scoops out a

Retreating Waterfall:

overhang
plunge pool

overhang breaks away
boulders pile up
undercutting of waterfall

as rock breaks off, the waterfall retreats

deep depression, called a plunge pool, at the base of the falls. Because the water always splashes on it, the rocky cliff face along the waterfall may also wear away, creating an overhang—and a hollow space behind it. Eventually, the overhang breaks away and the process of erosion begins to shape a new overhang.

of water pour over North America's Niagara Falls. The world's highest waterfall is Venezuela's Angel Falls. It is named for the pilot and explorer Jimmy Angel, who discovered the Falls in 1935. Its waters drop for a total of 3212 feet, or nearly two-thirds of a mile!

Some rivers flow over natural cliffs or rises known as hanging valleys. Glaciers are often responsible for these hanging valleys.

Angel Falls, Venezuela

The ice of a glacier deepens an existing river valley by wearing away rock and soil as the glacier slowly moves along. When the glacier retreats, the river's tributaries, or feeder streams,

Bridalveil Falls, Yosemite National Park, with hanging valley

end up being higher above the new, deeper riverbed. Bridalveil Falls, in California's Yosemite National Park, flows from just such a hanging valley.

WATCH YOUR STEP

NIAGARA FALLS ATTRACTS not only tourists, but daredevils as well. At least eight people have tried to ride over the falls in a barrel. Of the eight, only five survived.

Annie Edson Taylor
On October 24, 1901, she won fame but didn't make it over the falls.

WHAT IS THE NILE?

THE NILE RIVER of Africa is the longest river in the world. It is about 4132 miles long. The Nile is the only river in the world that begins near the equator and flows into a temperate zone. This great river runs from near the equator in the south through swamps, forests, and the deserts of northern Africa, finally emptying into the Mediterranean Sea in the north.

The Nile is actually made up of three different rivers. The Atbara River and the Blue Nile begin in the Ethiopian highlands. (During the dry season, the Atbara becomes merely a string of pools in its riverbed.) The White Nile originates in springs to the south of Lake Victoria, which borders on Tanzania, Uganda, and Kenya. The Blue Nile and the White Nile meet at Khartoum in the Sudan. The Atbara joins the Nile 200 miles farther downriver at Atbara, also in the Sudan.

In the 1800s, many brave explorers risked their lives to find the source of the Nile. For a while, Lake Victoria was

ANIMAL ACTS

◀

ONE OF THE WORLD'S largest living reptiles, the Nile crocodile, grows to be as long as 16 feet. The creature has been known to capture and eat people who are not careful!

THE HIDDEN CANYON

WHEN EGYPT'S Aswan High Dam was being built on the Nile River in the 1960s, geologists studied the area. Material brought up from holes drilled deep into the present riverbed showed that beneath the river is a buried canyon. It is cut into the underlying rock more than 1000 feet below the present level of the Nile Valley. Even more surprising is that the material brought up from the deepest holes originated in seawater!

It seems that about 5 million years ago, the Mediterranean Sea had been cut off from the Atlantic Ocean and had dried up. The Nile flowed more quickly then, and the rushing water carved out a deep canyon that dropped down to the level of the new Mediterranean Valley. When the Atlantic/Mediterranean link opened up again, the sea refilled and a branch of it worked its way up the ancient Nile Valley. Slowly but surely, the riverbed rose again. Over millions of years it deposited sand and mud in the canyon until it eventually filled to its present level.

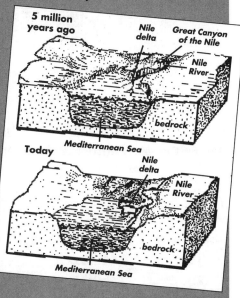

thought to be the source of the White Nile. In fact, the waters come from even farther south. Lake Victoria itself is fed by a small river called the Kagera. Two hundred fifty miles southwest of Lake Victoria, in Burundi, the Kagera is formed from 10 small mountain springs. This river then empties into Lake Victoria, and its current reaches as far as the lake's north shore, in Uganda, where the lake waters spill into the Nile. The German explorer who discovered where the Kagera began put up a plaque calling the place *Caput Nili*, Latin for "source of the Nile."

WRITE THAT DOWN!

▼

HISTORICALLY, THE NILE is a very important river. In addition to supplying the ancient Egyptians with water, it provided them with writing materials. The reeds of the papyrus, a grasslike plant that grows along the shores of the river, were used to make a form of paper, and stiff, sharpened reeds were used as pens.

WHAT IS THE AMAZON?

THE AMAZON RIVER is the mightiest river on Earth. It flows eastward across most of the South American continent and is nearly 4000 miles long. The Amazon is so deep and wide that large ships can travel nearly halfway across South America in its waters. Although it is not the world's longest river (the Nile in Africa is about 250 miles longer), the Amazon carries more water than any other river in the world. To be more exact, the Amazon carries 20 to 25 percent of all the earth's river water. The Amazon drainage basin (an area that includes the streams and smaller rivers that flow into the Amazon) covers more than one-third of the South American continent. It is eight times larger than the drainage basin of the Mississippi River of the United States. In fact, about 1100 rivers and streams flow into, or feed, the Amazon.

The Amazon contains at least 1300 species of fish, and perhaps as many as 2000. That's more species than in the entire Atlantic Ocean! The river water, however, is poor in nutrients. Water plants do not grow well, so some of these fish, including piranha, get their food from the surrounding forest. They swim close to the banks of the river waiting for leaves, seeds, and fruit to fall. When the river floods its banks and water flows into the forest, as it often does, the fish swim far into the forest and eat their fill! One thing that the Amazon doesn't have is a delta. A delta

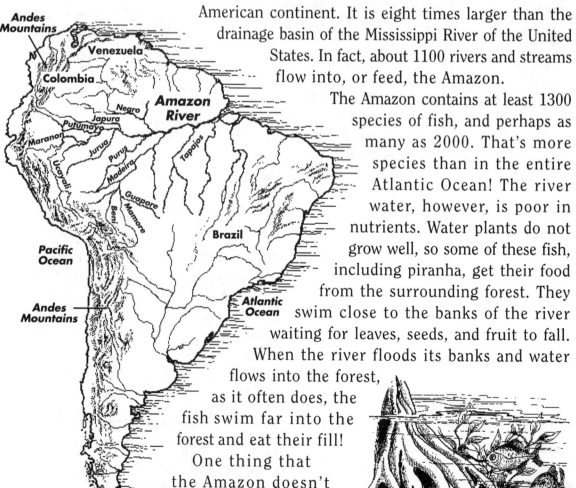

fruit-eating piranha

is an "island" of land that forms at the mouth of a river. Rivers carry fine sand and mud, known as silt, in their waters. When rivers reach a sea or ocean, the waters slow down and the silt drops out and builds up, layer upon layer, on the seafloor. The mud and silt of the Amazon cannot form a delta because the river is so powerful. Its rushing water does not slow down until it is more than *100 miles* out to sea! In fact, sailors in the Atlantic Ocean can see the Amazon River as a yellowish, muddy stream in the ocean waters long before they can see the coast of South America.

POISON OR MEDICINE?

CURARE (koo-RAH-ree) is a deadly poison that comes from plants growing along the Amazon. Curare has been used by the native peoples of the Amazon to tip their arrows (and is still used today in some areas). But curare is also used successfully in modern medicine to treat serious diseases such as multiple sclerosis and Parkinson's disease.

RECORD SETTERS

THE AMAZON RIVER is home to a number of remarkable creatures, including the following record-setters:

anaconda

- The anaconda, one of the world's largest snakes, grows to lengths of 35 feet or more.
- The arapaima (ar-uh-PY-muh), one of the world's largest freshwater fish, weighs in at about 200 pounds and may grow to 10 feet in length.
- The capybara (kap-ee-BAR-uh), the world's largest rodent, may grow to be 4 feet long and weigh 60 to 100 pounds.
- The pygmy marmoset, the world's smallest monkey, is a little more than 6 inches long, not counting its tail. That's smaller than a robin!

capybara

WHAT IS THE SARGASSO SEA?

THE SARGASSO SEA is the only major sea on Earth bordered entirely by ocean. The Sargasso's warm, clear waters cover around 2 million square miles of the North Atlantic Ocean, an area about half the size of the United States. It is the center of a huge gyre, or ring, of currents in the North Atlantic that includes the Gulf Stream, the North Atlantic Current, the Canaries Current, and the North Equatorial Current.

Although the ocean near the area of the Sargasso Sea is as much as 4 miles (or about 21,000 feet) deep, the Sargasso itself is no more than 3300 feet deep. And the water temperature remains warm, even in winter, averaging about 64 degrees. The sea floats on the colder water of the Atlantic Ocean much the same way that a patch of oil floats on water.

The borders of the Sargasso are determined by its salt content and temperature, both of which are much higher than most of the surrounding water of the Atlantic. Because the Sargasso Sea is located in an area that has few storms, and it receives only a little fresh water from rain, and through evaporation, it has become extremely salty.

Huge patches of a rootless brown seaweed, called sargassum, drift across the surface of the sea. They are kept afloat by pea-sized air-filled bladders.

Currents
1. North Atlantic
2. Gulf Stream
3. North Equatorial
4. Canaries
5. Antilles
6. Greenland
7. Brazil
8. Guinea

The sargassum is home to many different species of sea creatures. Tiny crabs and sea horses use the sargassum as a hiding place. Flying fish build nests in it to deposit their eggs. Tuna and marlin  also deposit their eggs there. The 8-inch-long sargassofish is especially dependent on the weed. One of the rare fish to sport prehensile (grasping) fins, it clings to the sargassum and pulls itself along in the water. Disguised to blend in with the weed, the sargassofish hides from enemies and waits in ambush for prey.

marlin

THE SARGASSO SEA was once known as the "graveyard of ships." Sailors thought that the seaweed spread over unfortunate vessels from end to end and held them in place. The sailors believed that this made them easy prey for sea monsters searching for a meal!

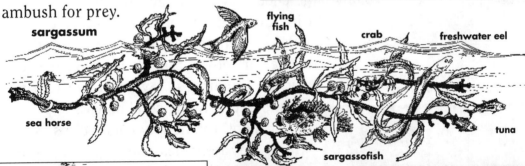

sargassum

flying fish

crab

freshwater eel

sea horse

sargassofish

tuna

United States

Bermuda

Bermuda Triangle

Cuba

Haiti

Dominican Republic

Puerto Rico

UNSOLVED MYSTERY ◄

IN AN AREA at the southwestern corner of the Sargasso Sea, various ships and planes carrying a total of more than 300 people have disappeared over the past 100 years without a trace. What's the name of this place? The Bermuda Triangle.

WHAT IS THE GREAT BARRIER REEF?

Arafura
Sea

Coral
Sea

Queensland

Great
Barrier
Reef

BRISBANE

SYDNEY

MELBOURNE

Queensland

BRISBANE

Tasman
Sea

THE GREAT BARRIER REEF of Australia is the world's longest and biggest coral reef. It is home to hundreds of different plants and animals. It is also one of the greatest structures ever built on Earth—and, remarkably, it was built by creatures no larger than the eraser on a pencil! The tiny animals, called coral polyps, are tube-shaped. They construct little cuplike, limestone shells for themselves using minerals extracted from seawater. The shell of each polyp is connected to others of its kind. In fact, a colony large enough to fill an average swimming pool would include billions of interconnected polyp shells. As individual polyps die, their shells become part of the base structure of the reef. Only the uppermost layers of the reef are composed of living coral polyps.

polyp, open and feeding at night

closed polyp

layers and layers of polyp shell build a coral reef

IT'S A FACT!

CORAL REEFS USUALLY form in warm waters of 75 degrees or more. Because the algae living on coral polyps need sunlight to make nutrients, living coral is always found in clear water that lets the sunlight through, and it is never more than 150 feet below sea level.

At night, the hungry coral polyps extend their tiny tentacles like fingers to trap a meal of plankton (microscopic plant and animal life floating in the water). They also obtain food from a special kind of single-celled algae that actually grows on the coral polyp. During the day, the algae uses sunlight and carbon dioxide (a waste product of the polyp) to produce sugars and starches. At night, these nutrients seep into the polyp and nourish it. For every square foot of living coral on the surface of the reef, there may be nearly *140 billion* of these tiny algae plants!

The Great Barrier Reef runs along Australia's northeastern coast for 1250 miles. In some places it is as much as 100 miles wide. In total, it covers nearly 90,000 square miles, an area roughly the size of the entire United Kingdom. In fact, it is so huge that the astronauts who landed on the Moon reported that it could be seen from there!

The giant Great Barrier Reef is not a continuous structure. It is actually made up of more than 2000 individual reefs. And while the coral polyps may be master builders, they are very slow builders. It has taken them between 20 and 30 *million* years to construct this amazing structure.

A LOT OF ROCK!

THE GREAT BARRIER REEF is made up of enough limestone to provide building blocks for 8 million structures the size of the largest Egyptian pyramid.

ANIMAL ACTS

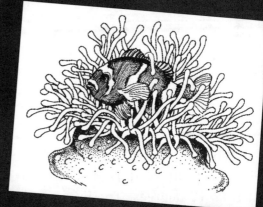

THE CLOWNFISH is an unusual resident of the reef. This small fish lives among the many stinging (and deadly) tentacles of sea anemones, simple reef animals that are distant relatives of the coral polyp. The clownfish feeds on scraps from the anemone's meals. As it does so, it relies on the anemone and its deadly tentacles to protect it from its enemies. But what protects the clownfish from the *anemone*? It seems that the sea anemone identifies its prey through touch and taste. To protect itself, the clownfish quickly brushes against the tentacles, coating itself with the anemone's own mucus. This mucus acts as a special shield and keeps the anemone from recognizing the clownfish as prey.

A TASTY MEAL ⇩

ONE OF THE animals that preys on living coral polyps is the parrotfish. With its strong jaws, it noisily munches on the soft bodies of the polyps, as well as on their hard limestone shells.

WHAT IS EL NIÑO?

EL NIÑO WAS the name originally used during the 1800s for the yearly mild warming of the surface of the Pacific Ocean along the western coast of South America. More recently, however, El Niño refers to the stronger warming that occurs every few years.

Normally, the surface waters off the coast of Peru and Ecuador are cool and full of plants and animals. That's because cold water full of nutrients comes up from deep in the ocean. As a result, plants can thrive, as can plant-eating sea creatures. With plenty of fish to eat, large fish and ocean birds also flock to the area. Each year, however, around the end of December, a warm current arrives. This current raises the surface temperature of the water by as much as 12 degrees. The warming lasts for only a few weeks, but it often brings heavy rains to Peru and Ecuador.

Every 5 to 7 years, however, the current is especially warm and it travels further to the south. And instead of staying just a few weeks, it often lingers for months. These unusual conditions, now known as El Niño, cause many changes. Certain local fish and birds leave the area, while new ones, attracted to the warmer water, take their place. El Niño can affect local weather conditions, too. For example, it may bring soaking rains to deserts. It can also have an affect on the weather thousands of miles from the shores it actually touches. In the South Pacific Ocean, the island of Tahiti had not suffered through a major storm during

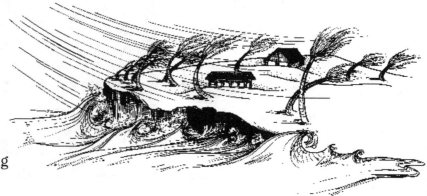

this century. But due to El Niño in 1982–1983, this small island was hit by 6 cyclones in 5 months!

How can all of this happen? El Niño results from changes in wind patterns. When wind patterns change, the movements of ocean water also change. The trade winds, which are bands of winds north and south of the equator, usually blow warm surface water west across the Pacific Ocean. As the warm water is blown away, the deeper, colder waters are exposed along the coast of South America. Every few years, however, the system that contributes to this normal wind pattern changes. The trade winds get weaker, and warm water is *not* blown away. Instead, it builds up in the central and eastern part of the Pacific Ocean. This weakens the trade winds even more, causing even more warm water to build up, and so on. Scientists are not yet certain what sets off this cycle, but by using computer technology, they can now predict it.

SNOW IN SUMMER

A VISIT FROM El Niño has been blamed for the bizarre weather that occurred in the Great Plains states of the United States in the early 1800s. In fact, 1816 was known as the year without a summer. Heavy snow fell in June, and one July blizzard lasted for three days.

EL NIÑO'S SISTER

VERY STRONG TRADE winds, causing unusually cold temperatures on the surface of the warm, tropical Pacific Ocean, are sometimes called La Niña. La Niña means "the girl child," and it, too, affects weather around the world. La Niña may have contributed to the recent drought in the southwestern United States during the summer of 1988.

El Niño
La Niña

WHAT IS THE GULF STREAM?

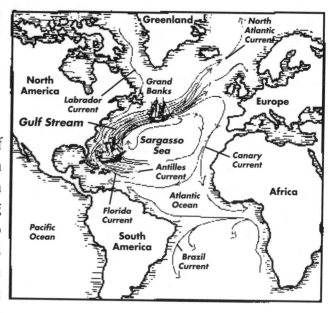

THE GULF STREAM is one of Earth's most powerful ocean currents. It forms the western boundary of a large gyre, or ring of currents, with the Sargasso Sea at its center. Ocean currents develop because the waters are not still. The ocean waters are shifted by tides and built up into huge waves by storm winds. And the constant, steady, global winds set up surface currents, which are a little like fast-flowing streams in the ocean.

The Gulf Stream is actually a system of currents that join together to form the main body of the current. The current begins in the warm waters of the 50-mile-wide Florida Straits. This Florida Current rushes between the Florida Keys and the islands of the Bahamas at about 4 miles per hour to as much as 10 miles per hour at its center. The amount of water passing through this area is at least 25 times that carried in all the world's rivers added together! When it reaches the Atlantic Ocean, the Florida Current is joined by the Antilles Current. Then at Cape Hatteras, off North Carolina, the Gulf Stream proper is formed. It continues flowing in a northeasterly direction along the east coast of the United States to the Grand Banks, an undersea area off Canada. At the Grand Banks, the Gulf Stream turns east and becomes part of the North Atlantic Current.

✏ SEE FOR YOURSELF

WINDS ARE A major cause of ocean currents. You can create your own current in a large, shallow, round bowl. Fill the bowl with water, and begin to blow across the water just above the rim. The movement of the water in the bowl is a simplified, small-scale example of what happens in the ocean. To see the motion more clearly, add a drop or two of food coloring to the "current" you have created.

Where the Gulf Stream meets water of different temperatures at its edge, great meanders, or bends, form. These meanders often wrap around and pinch off a section of water, called a core, and then go swirling away. To the north of the Gulf Stream, cold water wraps around a warm core, and the ring breaks off. The warm water at the center may be a foot or two higher than the cold water at the edges. To the south of the Gulf Stream, rings with cold cores form. These tend to be larger and last longer than the northern rings. Both types of rings are deep, and the motion at their borders may cause storms on the ocean floor far below. A ring may last from a few days to a few years before fading away.

BIO BIT

▼

IN 1770, THE American scientist Benjamin Franklin noted that American ships traveling from England to Rhode Island made the trip about two weeks faster than British ships sailing to New York from a point farther south in England. Franklin asked his cousin, a whaling captain, why this might be, and he was told the ships were traveling against a powerful current in the Atlantic Ocean. Franklin asked his cousin to map the current for him, and the first chart of the Gulf Stream was drawn.

AN INCREDIBLE JOURNEY

TO BETTER UNDERSTAND the movements of the great current, in 1969 oceanographer Jacques Piccard and his crew spent 30 days in a submarine drifting for 1500 miles within the Gulf Stream.

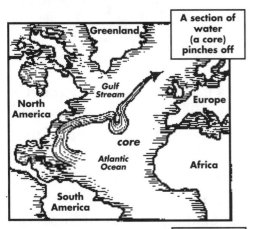

A section of water (a core) pinches off

Greenland

Gulf Stream

North America

Europe

core

Atlantic Ocean

Africa

South America

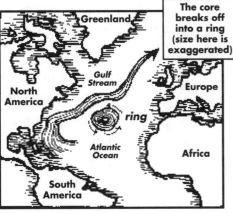

The core breaks off into a ring (size here is exaggerated)

Greenland

Gulf Stream

North America

Europe

ring

Atlantic Ocean

Africa

South America

WHAT IS A TSUNAMI?

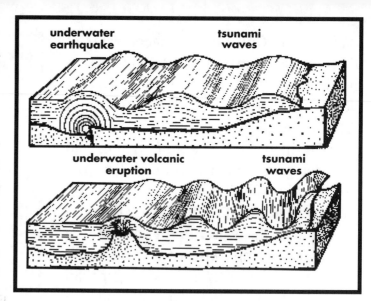

underwater earthquake — tsunami waves

underwater volcanic eruption — tsunami waves

A TSUNAMI (soo-NAH-mee) is a huge wave in the ocean caused by an underwater disturbance, such as a powerful earthquake, a volcanic eruption, or a landslide. Such a disturbance creates a series of waves much like the ripples that develop when a rock is thrown into a pool of water. But the waves are much larger!

The word *tsunami* is Japanese for "large waves in harbor." A tsunami may, in fact, be as tall as a 12-story building! And although tsunamis are sometimes called tidal waves, these powerful waves of water have nothing to do with the tides.

Far out in the ocean, where the water is very deep, a tsunami may travel at speeds of several hundred miles per hour, yet be only 2 or 3 feet high. Because the waves are so low, A ship at sea often does not notice them. In spite of their great speed, there may be anywhere from 5 minutes to an hour between one wave and the next. As a tsunami reaches shallower water near the shore, however, the wave changes significantly. It slows down and builds into a rushing wall of water that can be as high as 100 feet. As it smashes into the land, a tsunami can cause tremendous destruction. But unlike some disasters, a tsunami is fairly predictable. Once an undersea disturbance has been

WAVE OF DESTRUCTION

IN 1883, THE volcanic eruption of the island of Krakatoa sent a huge tsunami smashing into the islands of Java and Sumatra in Indonesia. More than 36,000 lives were lost. The power of the wave was clearly evident when a gunboat that had been anchored off the coast of Sumatra was discovered 2 miles inland!

reported, scientists carefully monitor changes in ocean conditions. Because of this, there are often several hours' warning, which gives people in a threatened area enough time to leave before the tsunami strikes.

The high point of a tsunami's wave (or any wave) is called the crest, and the lowest point between waves is called the trough. The trough of a tsunami may arrive at the shore before the crest of the wave. When that happens, the water level drops very quickly along the shore, and parts of the ocean floor are uncovered for a great distance. Tsunamis often come ashore in a series of eight or nine waves. The third and eighth waves are usually the largest. These waves come ashore anywhere from 15 minutes to an hour apart.

crest

trough

SPECIAL DELIVERY ▼

IN 1946, A tsunami caused by an earthquake near the Aleutian Islands off the coast of Alaska traveled 2000 miles in $4\frac{1}{2}$ hours. The wave was more than 50 feet high by the time it toppled over at the Hawaiian island of Kauai.

WAVE POWER

A LARGE TSUNAMI can have the destructive force of several million tons of dynamite!

WHAT IS A RAINBOW?

raindrop

incoming light

reflection

refraction

red
orange
yellow
green
blue
indigo
violet

A RAINBOW IS a beautifully colored curve, or arc, in the sky. A rainbow may appear when the sun breaks through the clouds after a rainstorm or thunderstorm. It is not something that can be touched, but is instead a trick of light. Usually rainbows last only a few minutes. But one sighted after a 1979 storm in Wales, in Great Britain, reportedly remained visible for more than three hours!

A rainbow is the result of sunlight being bent, or refracted, and then bounced back, or reflected, within raindrops. A glass prism can break sunlight into seven visible colors. Raindrops are like tiny prisms. As rays of sunlight enter a raindrop they are refracted toward the back of the raindrop, then reflected off the back toward the front. The rays are then bent again as they exit from the front of the raindrop. By then, the sunlight is separated into its seven individual colors, with each color leaving the raindrop at a slightly different angle.

Rainbows usually occur in the morning or afternoon because they cannot appear when the sun is too high in the sky. Because a rainbow is the result of

SEE FOR YOURSELF

ROYGBIV

WOULD YOU LIKE to try to break sunlight into its seven colors? You will need a tall glass, an index card, scissors, tape, and a large sheet of white paper. Cut a 1" by 3" rectangle from the center of the index card. Then tape the card to the side of the glass so half the opening is above the rim. Fill the glass with water and set it on a sunny windowsill. Put the white paper in the sunlight on the floor below. The water in the glass acts like a giant raindrop to break the sunlight that falls on the paper into its individual colors.

sunlight being bent by millions of raindrops at particular angles, and because no two people can stand in exactly the same place at the same time, no two people can ever see exactly the same rainbow. Sometimes there may even be two rainbows at once—a bright rainbow with a paler one above it. Double rainbows can occur when particularly large raindrops are present. They are caused when light in the raindrop is reflected not once, but twice. When that happens, the rays of sunlight leave the raindrop at a slightly different angle than when they bounce only once. In a double rainbow, the colors in the brighter arc, or primary bow, begin with a violet band on the bottom and end with a red band on the top. The colors in the paler arc, or secondary bow, are reversed, with violet at the top and red at the bottom.

A rainbow may be visible even on a rainless day. If the sun is behind you, it is possible to see a long-lasting rainbow in a light spray of water, such as the spray from a waterfall, a water fountain, or a garden hose. These rainbows are caused the same way as the rainbows that appear after a storm.

WHO IS HE?
▼

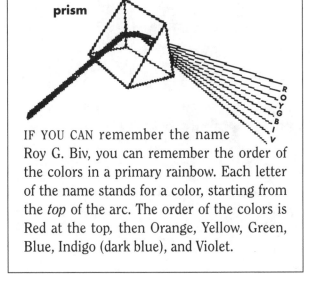

prism

IF YOU CAN remember the name Roy G. Biv, you can remember the order of the colors in a primary rainbow. Each letter of the name stands for a color, starting from the *top* of the arc. The order of the colors is Red at the top, then Orange, Yellow, Green, Blue, Indigo (dark blue), and Violet.

WHAT WAS ONCE BELIEVED
▼

THERE ARE MANY legends and myths about rainbows. The Greeks once believed a rainbow was the path taken by the goddess Iris, a messenger of the gods. To the Nordic peoples, the rainbow was known as Bifrost, a bridge that connected the home of the gods to the human world.

the Greek goddess Iris

WHAT IS A MIRAGE?

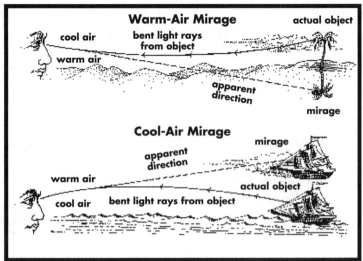

Warm-Air Mirage
cool air
warm air
bent light rays from object
actual object
apparent direction
mirage

Cool-Air Mirage
apparent direction
warm air
cool air
bent light rays from object
mirage
actual object

A MIRAGE IS an illusion that fools the eye by producing a false image. A mirage may be a false image of a real object that appears to be closer than it actually is. It may also be an illusion of something that doesn't exist at all. Have you ever seen water shimmering on the ground or on a highway ahead of you and then found that it was not really there? The water was a mirage—a mirror image of the blue sky.

A mirage is caused when light waves in the atmosphere are bent and then bounced back to the eye so that a double image appears. In the atmosphere, air of different temperatures forms layers. In a hot desert or on a sunlit highway, heat rising from the ground can form a thin layer of warm air very near the ground. Above this warm layer is a layer of cooler air. Light passing through one air layer to another is bent toward the colder air layer. For example, in the desert, some of the light reflected from a tree travels directly to your eye, and the true image of the tree is seen. Some of the reflected tree light is also directed toward the ground. There, it is bent away from the warm air and toward the

IT'S A FACT!

MIRAGES can be photographed!

← SEE FOR YOURSELF

TO SEE HOW light waves bend in a mirage, perform the following experiment. Fill a glass with water. Drop a pencil in the glass, then look at it from the side. The pencil will look bent, but of course it isn't. Rather, it is the *light* that bends as it moves from the air layer above to the water layer below.

OUTRAGEOUS!

THE FATA MORGANA is a famous mirage that appears in Italy over a body of water called the Straits of Messina. The mirage is a stack of three villages piled one on top of the other in the sky. Several air layers of different temperatures all sandwiched together cause this strange image. As light passes through one layer of air to the next, it is bent several times. You see a right-side-up image on top of an upside-down image on top of a right-side-up image!

BIO BIT

THE BRITISH EXPLORER Sir John Ross was among the many people who searched for the Northwest Passage, a water route that was believed to connect the Atlantic and Pacific Oceans north of Canada. In 1818, Ross sailed into Lancaster Sound in northern Canada, hoping to discover such a route. He was sadly disappointed. A huge mountain range was blocking his way. He gave up, but he shouldn't have. The mountains were a mirage!

cooler air above. Because this bent light reaches your eye from a different angle, a mirage image of the tree, an upside-down one, is seen below the real tree.

Mirages may appear at sea as well, particularly where the water is very cold. At sea, the layer of air closest to the water is usually cooler than the layer of air above it. Because the layering of the air over cool water is different from that in hot areas, a mirage at sea differs from a land mirage. A sea mirage appears right side up and *above* the object. For example, light waves traveling upward from a distant ship are bent downward when they reach the warmer air layer above. To an observer, this creates a double image. The real ship is seen on the ocean, with a mirage image sailing right side up in the sky above the true ship.

IT'S A FACT!

▼

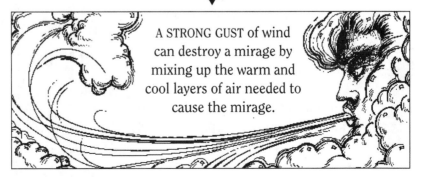

A STRONG GUST of wind can destroy a mirage by mixing up the warm and cool layers of air needed to cause the mirage.

WHAT IS LIGHTNING?

LIGHTNING IS A tremendous electrical spark that flashes from cloud to cloud or between a cloud and the ground. Scientists are not exactly certain how lightning forms. One theory is that within a storm cloud, ice and water droplets are blown up and down by powerful winds. Charged positive and negative particles in the cloud separate. The positive particles move to the top of the cloud. The negative ones sink to the bottom, causing the lower part of the cloud to become negatively charged. Since opposite charges attract each other, the negative particles in the storm cloud become attracted to the positively charged ground below the storm. Lightning is the energy released when a huge number of charged particles join, creating a flash of electrical current.

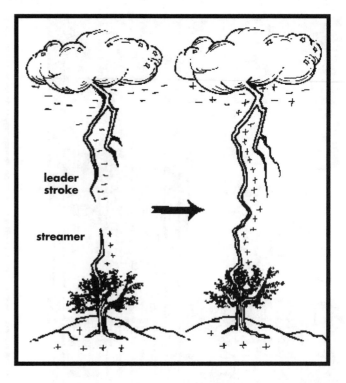

leader stroke

streamer

Air (particularly dry air) is a poor conductor, which means that it usually resists the flow of electricity. However, as the negative charge builds up in the cloud, the electric charge becomes powerful enough to overcome the resistance of the air. First, a *leader stroke* travels downward from the cloud for about 100 feet. It pauses and then continues earthward,

IT'S A FACT!

A SINGLE FLASH of lightning may reach temperatures almost five times hotter than the surface of the sun. And although a single flash lasts for only a few millionths of a second, it can pack enough energy to run a 100-watt light bulb for three months! ◀

GOOD ODDS

ONLY ONE IN five lightning bolts actually touches the ground.

creating a slender channel from the cloud almost to the ground. Then a *streamer* rises from the positively charged ground to meet the leader. When the leader and streamer join, an electrical circuit is completed. A *return stroke* then surges upward back toward the cloud, thus producing a flash of lightning. A single flash may be made up of as many as 20 individual return strokes.

Thunder is the very loud noise created by the rapid heating and expanding of air by lightning. The reason we see lightning before we hear the thunder it creates is that light travels much faster than sound. To determine how far away lightning is, count the number of seconds between the flash of lightning and the sound of thunder. Then divide that number by five (because it takes about five seconds for sound to travel one mile). The result is how many miles away the lightning occurred.

ENOUGH IS ENOUGH

DURING ONE STORM, New York City's Empire State building was struck by lightning 12 times in 20 minutes.

WHAT WAS ONCE BELIEVED
▼

THOR WAS THE Norse god of thunder. According to legend, Thor caused storms when he blew into his wild red beard and created thunder and lightning with a huge hammer called Miolnir.

SAFETY FIRST

IT'S BEST NOT to use the telephone, sit close to the television, or take a bath or shower during a lightning storm. Ground current from a nearby strike can travel through pipes, phone lines, and electric lines and cause serious injury to a person.

WHAT IS A TORNADO?

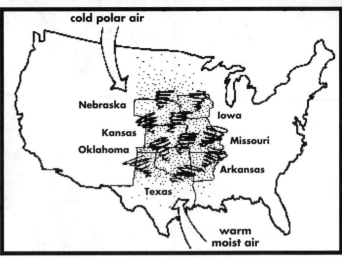

A TORNADO IS a tall tunnel of rapidly rotating air that extends from a cloud to the ground. It is one of the most powerful and unpredictable of nature's storms. Tornadoes occur in many parts of the world, but the greatest number of these storms—and some of the fiercest—roar through an area of the United States known as "Tornado Alley." This wide area includes parts of Texas, Oklahoma, Kansas, Nebraska, Iowa, Missouri, and Arkansas. The area is hit by at least 300 and as many as 700 tornadoes every year.

Tornadoes generally form in late spring, when warm, moist air moving up from the Gulf of Mexico meets cool, dry air that flows across the Rocky Mountains or moves down from Canada. In late afternoon, the ground begins to release the heat absorbed during the day. The warm air rises, creating an updraft, and the moisture in the air condenses into clouds. The cooler air sinks, creating a downdraft and forming what is known as a storm cell. As storm cells develop, a dark, flat-topped thundercloud swells upward. If the system holds together, it becomes a huge supercell, which may rise as high as 10 miles into the atmosphere. It is from such supercells as these that tornadoes are born.

Some scientists suspect that differences in wind speeds may

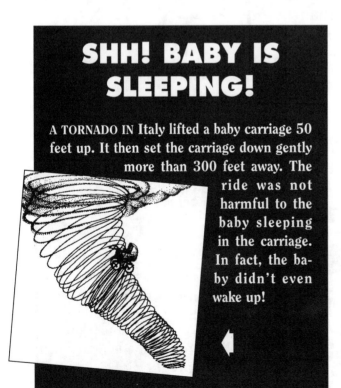

SHH! BABY IS SLEEPING!

A TORNADO IN Italy lifted a baby carriage 50 feet up. It then set the carriage down gently more than 300 feet away. The ride was not harmful to the baby sleeping in the carriage. In fact, the baby didn't even wake up!

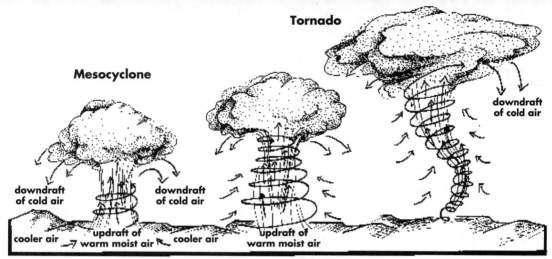

Mesocyclone

Tornado

downdraft
of cold air

downdraft
of cold air

downdraft
of cold air

cooler air · updraft of warm moist air · cooler air · updraft of warm moist air

cause the air around the center of the storm cloud to rotate at up to 60 miles per hour. This rotating air is called a mesocyclone. Next, a dark curtain called a wall cloud drops threateningly earthward. In extremely powerful storm clouds, the rotation of the mesocyclone creates a whirling funnel cloud that snakes lower and lower down from the sky. The funnel cloud may be between 300 and 2000 feet tall. Once in contact with the ground, it is called a tornado. Tornado winds are the fastest on Earth, reaching speeds of 300 miles or more per hour.

The forward rate of travel of the tornado itself is anywhere from 30 miles per hour to as much as 100 miles per hour! Few tornadoes last more than 30 minutes. An exception to this was a 1917 tornado in Texas that lasted for 7 hours and traveled nearly 300 miles.

PRETTY RUDE

IN 1950, A tornado in Bedfordshire, England, caught several chickens by surprise. The birds survived, but the storm stripped them of their feathers. ➡

HOW WEIRD!

TORNADOES SPIN clockwise in the Southern Hemisphere but counterclockwise in the Northern Hemisphere. ➡

North America

Northern Hemisphere

equator

Southern Hemisphere

South America

WHAT ARE THE POLES?

THERE ARE TWO parts to this answer, because the Earth has two sets of poles. One set of poles is the geographic poles. The other set is the magnetic poles. The geographic poles and magnetic poles are not at the same place on Earth.

The geographic poles are the northernmost and southernmost points on Earth. The southern geographic pole in Antarctica is on land. The northern geographic pole is over the Arctic Ocean. These poles are used as reference points by sailors, pilots, or anyone who needs to figure out their location anywhere on the Earth. Locations are determined using a grid of lines that measure distance in units, called degrees. Horizontal lines, called parallels, circle the globe from the equator to each pole. These lines are used to measure latitude, which is the distance north and south of the equator. Meridians are vertical lines that stretch from pole to pole. These lines are used to determine longitude, which is the distance east and west of a line called the prime meridian, which passes through Greenwich, England.

The magnetic poles are the two points from which Earth's magnetic field sweeps out from the planet in huge curves, or arcs. Like a bar magnet, the Earth is surrounded by a magnetic field, which is the area around Earth where magnetic forces can be observed. Earth's magnetic field is called the magnetosphere. The magnetosphere protects the Earth from dangerous radiation, such as X rays and ultraviolet rays from the solar wind. The solar wind is the continuous flow of particles from the sun. It comes in contact with the magnetosphere about 40,000 miles from Earth. There,

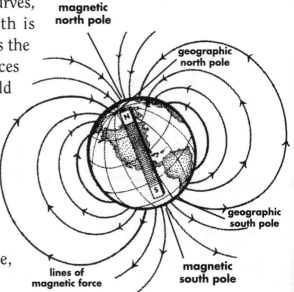

the solar wind parts and streams around the magnetosphere. Although visible light from the sun gets through to the Earth, most of the harmful rays do not. Some radiation, however, finds its way into the openings at the magnetic poles known as the polar cusps. When this radiation enters Earth's atmosphere, it produces the magnificent auroras, which are glowing curtains of colored light that may be seen in the polar night sky.

The Earth's Magnetosphere

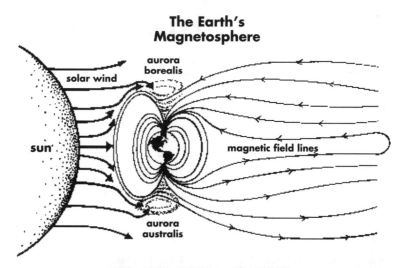

ON THE MOVE

THE GEOGRAPHIC POLES are always in the same place on Earth. The magnetic poles, however, do not stay in exactly the same place. They move around as much as a mile each year. Generally, the north magnetic pole is near Baffin Island, Canada. The south magnetic pole is near an area of Antarctica called Victoria Land.

POLAR RINGS

▼

AT THE NORTH pole, the glowing colored light in the night sky is called the *aurora borealis,* which in Latin means "northern dawn." At the South Pole, it is called the *aurora australis,* or "southern dawn." We know them better as the northern and southern lights. Though auroras look like curtains of light, if you could see an entire aurora you would see it is a ring of glowing air above the poles.

GLOSSARY

ALGAE Simple, water-living plants that have no leaves, roots, or stems. The singular of *algae* is *alga*.

CANYON A deep, steep-sided opening in the Earth's surface. A canyon is usually cut through rock by the action of rushing river water.

CURRENT The flow of a gas or liquid in a particular direction. The Gulf Stream is a current of water in the Atlantic Ocean. Currents of air are felt as wind.

EROSION The wearing away of land and rocks by natural forces, such as the action of wind and water. The word "erode" is from the Latin word *rodere*, meaning "to gnaw."

EVAPORATION The change of a liquid to a gas through the movement of air or through heating. Wind movement and the warmth of the sun cause water to evaporate from lakes, rivers, and seas.

EVOLUTION The gradual change in the traits of a species that make the species better able to survive in its existing environment or in a changing environment.

FISSURE A narrow but deep crack or opening in the surface of the Earth's crust.

FOSSIL The remains, trace, or impression of a once-living plant or animal preserved in rock.

GLACIER A huge mass of ice that moves slowly downhill under its own weight. Glaciers are made up of snow that builds up in cold areas, such as on mountaintops. Over many years, the weight of the upper layers of snow presses down on the lower layers, turning them to ice.

GROUNDWATER Water that is found beneath the surface of the Earth.

MAGMA Extremely hot, melted, rocky material that is found beneath the Earth's crust. During a volcanic eruption, magma may reach the surface of the Earth in the form of lava.

MINERAL A natural substance found in the ground that, with few exceptions, does not come from plants or animals. Rocks are made up of one or more minerals. Gold, iron, and sulfur are minerals.

PERMAFROST A permanently frozen layer of soil. Permafrost is often found in areas that were once covered by glaciers.

PLANKTON Tiny, sometimes microscopic forms of plant and animal life that drift in Earth's seas and oceans. Many ocean animals rely on plankton for food.

PLATEAU A flat-topped or slightly rounded area of land that is raised higher than the surrounding land.

POLLEN Tiny grains produced by a flower that contain the male reproductive cells of the plant.

POROUS Describes a material that has tiny pits or pores in it, making the material capable of absorbing water or allowing water to pass through it.

SALINITY The salt content of a substance, such as seawater.

TRIBUTARY A stream or small river that empties into a larger river or lake.

VENT An opening or hole in the Earth's crust through which gas, liquids, or other material may reach the surface. Lava may reach the surface of the Earth through volcanic vents. Streams of magma-heated water may enter the ocean through hydrothermal vents on the seafloor.

INDEX